THE

# REALITIES

OF

# EXISTENCE

UNVEILING THE EXISTENCE OF
INVISIBLE REALITIES. NEVER TO BE
CAUGHT UNAWARES OF WHAT LIES
AHEAD.

_____

**NIOLA IJAD**

**The Realities of Existence**
**Copyright** © March 2022 Niola Ijad
All rights reserved.


Published by: Goodnews World Publications.
Info@goodnews-world.org

*Unless otherwise indicated, Scripture quotations are taken from the Holy Bible, New Living Translation, copyright 1996, 2004, 2007 by Tyndale House Foundation. Used by permission of Tyndale House Publishers, incorporated. Carol Stream, Illinois 60188. All rights reserved and The King James Version of the Bible.*

Niola Ijad Production 2022


ISBN: 9798807107879

\*\*\*\*\*\*

# DEDICATION

This book is dedicated to the Spirit of the Ancient of Days who has been inspiring me to write this eye-opening book, taking me through the mysteries and wonders of creations, both seen and unseen.

Thank you, my Best Friend, my Helper, my Leader, Guide and Director. Thank You for using me as a vessel in Your hands. Thank You for staying with me through this beautiful piece. Thank You for taking me through Your school. You are so amazing. I couldn't have written this piece without Your divine inspiration.

# APPRECIATION

\*\*\*\*\*\*

# Contents

# INTRODUCTION

The Ancient clock keeps ticking on. Hours keep rolling by, hour after hour, and in the hours of his clock are mysteries, that are yet to be unveiled to many. "The Realities of Existence" brings to light, the many invisible events that are invariably occurring in the spiritual world. This book is particularly targeted towards channelling readers to various occurrences that are lined up for the human race in this world and in the worlds beyond. Many are oblivious to the reality of Life.

The Realities of Existence also brings to light, the components of the human nature and the reality of existence that surrounds them. It is of utmost importance for every human being on earth to understand who they are; that is, their components, personal existence and the reality of existence that surrounds them. This does not refer to the components that make up the
physical human body, but that of the human nature. Only then would they be able to understand how to process themselves on their journey on earth, according to the truth unveiled. Imagine setting a passcode to your device, with no one being able to get into your device except through your passcode.

My Master has been teaching and enlightening me through His Spirit in amazing ways. He has revealed and unfolded secrets of events to me, and I am inviting you to follow me on this beautiful journey in the unfolding of events. I am simply a vessel in the hands of my Master. I am grateful to Him for giving me the opportunity of sharing with you, the mystery of events through the pages of this invaluable book.

Most assuredly, you will discover much truth unveiled to you from the contents of this book, which will certainly bring you to a desired haven. I do hope you would find these pages inspiring.

Niola Ijad.

# Chapter 1

## THE INVISIBLE SIDE OF LIFE

Has it ever occurred to you, that life extends beyond this natural world in which we live? Many events are taking place behind the curtains of this present world and it will ever take beyond our natural self to discover these things. Some people, already are active participants in the invisible events that lay beyond this present world, whilst some are not even aware of the events that lay ahead of them in the very near future and in the times to come. They have no clue, no knowledge or insight of what is happening behind the curtains of this very present earthly world. Either you or I know it or not, does not remove the reality of these many events that we all are yet to encounter. My question today is, are you seeing beyond this physical realm into the realm of spiritual events that lay beyond our earthly world?

Presently, our physical eyes have the ability to behold the wondrous beauty of God's creations and the creativity of His creatures, but to see beyond this world will ever take our unseen or spiritual eyes to peer through. This is the truth and reality that we all need to be aware of. It is of utmost importance that every individual begins to recognise themselves firstly, as a Spirit Being who is actually on a spiritual journey and has many choices to make with regards the keeping of their soul and spirit man.

The real and substantial things that lay ahead of each one of us are quite invisible, but are of a reality, and of great importance to our very existence. Many events lay invisibly beyond the world in which we presently live in, of which our physical eyes cannot comprehend, except we discover them with the eyes of our spirit. Every human being on earth is a spirit being, having a soul and living in a body. The reality is that: *An individual's spirit is either dead and oblivious or awake and alive to the invisible side of life with a glimpse of its realities.*

The good news is that, at the point where a person's spirit is made alive, they become aware of the existence of another kingdom and another life. The experience is like that of newly born babe arriving into the physical world. From the moment of time, that a person's spirit is made alive, it becomes automatically connected to another side of life. They become vividly aware of the existence of another kingdom, lined up with so many exciting events.

# Chapter 2

## THE SPIRITUAL SIDE OF LIFE

The creation of Life is quite vast and mysterious, and too large for our human hearts to comprehend. On the other hand, the existence of spiritual life is not only vast and mysterious to us, but can never be understood with the natural mind. It sounds foolish to every natural man. The spiritual side of life cannot be seen with the physical eyes, because it is invisible, and a spiritual world in itself. However, for everyone that would step into this invisible world of glory, grace and honour; there would always be a knowing in their Inner Man, beyond every doubt of their translation into a glorious and timeless world.

It is with one's spirit that a person can be in touch with the spiritual world. Therefore, communication with the spiritual world can never be achieved with the human body or natural mind, but with the spirit of man. Adequately explained in this book, is how an individual can be in touch with the spiritual realm, by the awakening of their Inner Man. We all, as individuals, have the opportunity of not only coming to the knowledge of the spiritual side of life, but actually having an experience of the spiritual life in itself.

This ancient, timeless, pure, glorious and exquisite kingdom is filled with so many treasures and riches untold, made available to as many who are able to find their way in, through its doors. However, just like a miner would have to dig deep beyond the surface of the earth in order to retrieve the substance of gold, they that enter in, would also have to dig deep beyond the surface of this present earthly world, into the ageless world of grace and glory, in order to discover the many treasures that the creator of the universe has put into place for them and the entire human race.

This world in which we live in is only a mirror and reflection of the invisible side of life.  We all need to come to the understanding that the existence of life is more real and tangible on the spiritual side of life than on the natural side of life.  Our natural life is a shadow of our spiritual life! This is the reason why the creator of the universe said "Now we see things imperfectly, like puzzling reflections in a mirror, but then we will see everything with perfect clarity.  All that I know now is partial and incomplete, but then I will know everything completely, just as God now knows me completely."  (1 Corinthians 13:12).

# Chapter 3

## THE TRIPARTITE MAN

The aspect of the three-fold nature of man is in itself a vast and voluminous subject to discuss. However, in this book, I shall only be making a brief description of the Tripartite Man, which is the three-fold nature of a human existence.

For awareness purposes and a better understanding, I would love to start this particular topic by first helping to define our human tripartite nature. We all, as individuals, are three-fold in nature; that is the Spirit, Soul and Body, which operate on three different dimensions. It is very vital if you can think of yourself firstly as a Spirit Being, who possesses a soul and lives in a body rather than a body with a soul, as many people would have thought.

The body is the third part of the threefold nature and can best be described as the lowest segment of the human existence, and in the third dimension of its creation. It is the only visible part of an individual. It is also the Natural Man part of the human existence, and spiritual things sound foolish to him. (1Corinthians 2:14). The body, referred to as the outward man, can be likened to a house that accommodates the spirit and the soul. With the body, we see, hear, feel, touch and make contact generally with the world. The body connects and relates with the physical activities of this world and would normally play along with the dictates of both the spirit and soul of man, respectively.

Every individual on earth lives in a physical body which will eventually become old, and when it dies, it will have every tendency to physically decompose, or otherwise be cremated. The body is the corruptible segment of human life. At death, the body will fall off like a jacket and will be replaced immediately with an incorruptible jacket-body for the spirit and soul to put on. In actual fact, what we refer to as death, is just the falling away of the Jacket-house from the spirit and soul of a person, to be replaced with an incorruptible jacket, which is immortal, and fit for living in the next eternal abode. At death, all three-fold nature - spirit, soul and immortal body of such individual becomes invisible and unseen to the natural man still living on earth. It is very important to understand that when a person dies, they are indeed still very much alive, but in a different realm. However, all we see of a dead person is what we refer to as the corpse, which is the old jacket. This is a very solid truth. Trying to dispute this truth will be like trying to deny the existence of air being breathed in and out because it cannot be seen. God tells us in His word: "For this corruptible must put on incorruptible, and this mortal must put on immortality. So, when this corruptible shall have put on incorruptible, and this mortal shall have put on immortality, then shall be brought to pass the saying that is written, "Death is swallowed up in victory." (1 Corinthian 15:53-54).

The scriptures also mentioned that: "For which reason, we faint not; but though our outward man perish, yet the inward man is renewed day by day." (2 Corinthians 4:16). At death, the spirit and soul detach themselves from the body immediately but, we must recognize and consider this, as only a transition of an individual from one place to another.

The Soul is the second part of the threefold nature, and in the second dimension of man's threefold nature. It is non-material and the unseen part inside of an individual that makes them the unique individual that they are. The soul of man can be referred to as the mind and deals with the mental realm. It is the part of man that reasons and thinks. Science refers to this as the Psychic area of man. The soul produces expressions of feelings, will, and emotions. Human beings contact the intellectual realm with the soul. This is not with reference to the physical human components here, but of the human nature. Therefore, I am not referring to the brain component part of the body. In the context of this discussion, the brain can be referred to as an organ in the third dimensional body part of man, that helps in coordinating this second dimensional mental realm part of the soul. We cannot say that the soul is the highest or lowest part of the threefold nature of human existence, but it operates at a higher level than the body and at a much lower level than the spirit of man.

The mental faculty has been responsible for the many activities that humans carry out on a daily basis in various aspects of life. It is the producer or introducer of the many events and vast creativity that surround us in our environments, whilst the Body is like the machinery which carries out or manufactures events according to the dictates or the intents of this soulish part of Man.

The soulish part of an individual, however *intelligent*, is naturally *untamed* and will accommodate and entertain evil of the highest order wherever possible, resulting in disorderliness, chaos, corruption, instability, and a host of unpredictable characteristics in society. It is only by the power of the *re-birth* of the *Spirit* that a Soul can be brought to order.

13

The Spirit of the human being, known as The Spirit Man, is the first part of the threefold nature. The Spirit Man is the real person who we really are and equally invisible. It is referred to as the inward invisible man, however, more real than our physical body. To be precise, each person on earth is a Spirit, living in a body and having a soul. With our spirit, we are able to make contact with God, and the spiritual world.

Our spirit being is the highest part of us, and has the potential of having an upper hand over the soul and body alike. It is the decision maker, which can bring about various responses and actions from our soul and body. In order for our physical body to be able to function here on earth, our spirit man equally has to be alive in us here on earth.

We cannot know or relate with God mentally because He is Spirit. Likewise, we cannot relate physically with God or touch Him because He is not a human being, but Spirit Being. We can only communicate and reach God with our spirit. Our spirit being part of us therefore, is that which connects and relates with God. It is only through our spirit that we can truly get to know God, hence the importance of the rebirth of the spirit being part of us.

Just as the physical human body has the potential to grow up into a fully developed person, likewise, the soul has the ability to develop *intellectually*, and the *regenerated* Spirit of man has the potential to grow up spiritually without limits. The physical body however, grows in structure and has its limits, and after reaching its limits, it begins to decline. The soul operates in the realm of the mind, and has the potential to grow in creativity, intelligence, wisdom, knowledge and understanding. However, all of its characteristics are limited to earthly wisdom. At *rebirth,* the Spirit Man is born young and immature, but it has every potential to grow into maturity in the ways, and in the principles of God. The Spirit Man can grow in the grace and knowledge of God, and as it continues to grow, it climbs higher into the supernatural realms of God and is able to operate at a much higher level in God without limits.

The *regenerated* Spirit Man has the potential of tapping into the supernatural realms of God, to receive supernatural providence of various kinds for himself and for those whom he will impact, by the power of his faith in God. It is the Spirit Man part of the human nature that hears the voice of God, when He speaks. The regenerated Spirit Man is also able to move from one level of glory to another level continuously, into the fullness of God. At that point, he is able to operate very effectively in the supernatural. It is that part of him which has the potential to operate in the supernatural and gain dominion over sin, sicknesses, oppression, works of darkness, demons, rulers of darkness, spiritual wickedness, principalities and powers of darkness. The Spirit Man is also able to receive supernatural gifts from God and operate the gifts given to him on a supernatural dimension, without having learnt them. Although, one can be trained on how to channel the operations of the gifts appropriately.

When a re-birth occurs in a person, firstly, the power of the evil nature is broken from the human life, by the power of the Holy Spirit who comes to take up residence in the spirit of such individual, by way of the Blood of Jesus Christ. The spirit of such person then becomes alive. He or she becomes Born Again, and gets connected to God. The spirit part of this person begins to realise how wrong it had lived all along. He or she begins to walk in the newness of the birth received. This person begins to receive instructions from God and begins to understand the ways of God.

15

And also begins to understand truth. A transformation begins to take place from within the Spirit Man. It is important to note that this is not the same as reformation. Reformation is a man-made effort to change or improve on oneself. Transformation of the Spirit Man is a miracle from God to man. It involves the complete conversion or transition of the sinful heart condition of man, into a godly heart disposition. The spirit that has received Christ Jesus then begins to emit light into the dark parts of the soul, sending the truth that he or she has heard from the heavenly Father through the written word and every other source of truth to its soul. The Spirit of such person begins to see the productions of its soul's shortcomings and allows it to be cleansed through the washing of God's Word. The soul or mind begins to be renewed by the cleansing of God's Word which in return begins to send messages to the body on how to comport itself in a godly manner.

It is worthy to note and understand that, God in heaven particularly created each one of us as an eternal being. Every death of all human beings is in fact a transition of the human spirit into eternity, whereby they put off the physical body and put on an eternal or celestial body which is immortal, hence each one of us is able to continue living in eternity.

God has made Jesus Christ to be our perfect example when He said: "And as concerning that he raised him up from the dead, now no more to return to corruption, he said on this wise, I will give you the sure mercies of David. Wherefore, he said also in another Psalm, "You shall not suffer your Holy one to see corruption". For David, after he had served his own generation by the will of God, fell on sleep, and was laid unto his fathers, and saw corruption: But he, whom God raised again, saw no corruption." (Acts 13:34-37).

Jesus Christ is the first Born amongst many regenerated or re-birthed individuals. (Romans 8:29). These ones are referred to as the redeemed. The bible talks about Jesus Christ being raised from death on the third day. Jesus Christ was raised up in spirit and soul, after which He put on an immortal body. God allowed this to happen in order to demonstrate the importance of the death of Jesus Christ, and also to raise many who would believe in His death and resurrection, who would be planted in Christ Jesus, allowing them to also experience resurrection unto eternal life, at the instance of physical death. Jesus Christ passed through death for three days before resurrection. All glory be to God almighty! We would not have to make a journey of three days before resurrection. This is the reason why Jesus cried "It is finished" whilst he still hung on the cross. He had shed His blood for mankind and experienced resurrection at death. Halleluiah!

"But someone may ask, "How will the dead be raised? What kind of bodies will they have?" What a foolish question! When you put a seed into the ground, it doesn't grow into a plant unless it dies first. And what you put in the ground is not the plant that will grow, but only a bare seed of wheat or whatever you are planting. Then God gives it the new body he wants it to have. A different plant grows from each kind of seed. Similarly, there are different kinds of flesh – one kind for humans, another kind for animals, another for birds, and another for fish. There are also bodies in the heavens and bodies on the earth. The glory of the heavenly bodies is different from the glory of the earthly bodies. The sun has one kind of glory, while the moon and stars each have another kind. And even the stars differ from each other in their glory. It is the same way with the resurrection of the dead. Our earthly bodies are planted in the ground when we die, but they will be raised to live forever. Our bodies are buried in brokenness, but they will be raised in glory. They are buried in weakness, but they will be raised in strength.  They are buried as natural human bodies, but they will be raised as spiritual bodies.  For just as there are natural bodies, there are also spiritual bodies.  The scripture tells us, "The first man, Adam, became a living person."  But the last Adam – that is, Christ – is a life – giving Spirit.  What comes first is the natural body, then the spiritual body comes later.  Adam, the first man, was made from the dust of the earth, while Christ, the second man, came from heaven.  Earthly people are like the earthly man, and heavenly people are like the heavenly man.  Just as we are now like the earthly man, we will someday be like the heavenly man.  What I am saying, dear brothers and sisters, is that our physical bodies cannot inherit the kingdom of God.  These dying bodies cannot inherit what will last forever.  (1 Corinthian 15:35-50)

One prayer from God's word to us says in 1 Thessalonians 5:23: "Now may the God of peace himself sanctify you completely, and may your whole spirit and soul and body be kept blameless at the coming of our Lord Jesus Christ."  Therefore, the aspirations of each one of us ought to be, to be kept blameless until the day we face eternity.

# Chapter 4

## FORCES OF LIFE

God is real, Jesus is real, the Holy Spirit is real and the angels are real. All celestial beings are real; but, just like the wind is real, and indisputably invisible and you've never for once doubted the existence of wind, likewise, all of these aforementioned are invisible, and are eternal beings. The fact that you do not see them does not mean they are non-existence. The fact that you cannot see your spirit does not make you non-existence as a spirit being. Hence, you are eternal – never dying.

In the same vein, devils are real, but invisible, and some people have seen the manifestations of these beings in the lives of others and many of their deeds all over the world today. Some people refer to these beings as negative forces. These invisible beings can gain influence over the lives of people when care is not taken. Invisible as they are, they seek to supernaturally control individual lives and the human race at large. They influence thoughts, and actions of people, bringing about so much chaos upon our present world.

You need to be aware that there are different kingdoms in the universe – both visible and invisible. The ones you and I cannot see are undoubtedly more real. The truth I am trying to set across to you is that, even though you exist in your body, in the natural world, and pay attention to the visible world; it is essential that you also pay attention to the invisible world because you are eternal, and one day your physical body will perish at some point or the other, causing you to translate immediately into the invisible world, whilst the physical part of you is committed to dust or cremated. Hence, the eternal part of you will continue to live on.

The question you would want to ask yourself is, "where would I want to spend my eternity"? Every single person on earth is living on the edge of eternity every single day; and it is either on the edge of Eternal Damnation or Eternal Life. At the instance of physical death, you will find yourself going into the direction of where your feet find you at the close of your eyes in physical death. Many have opened their eyes only to face the reality that they never wanted to face and deal with whilst on earth. You see, this is the reason why you must ensure that the rebirth or regeneration of your spirit occurs.

# Chapter 5

## THE REBIRTH

Firstly, let's take a look at the use of these words. "I have experienced a *rebirth;* therefore, I have become *Born Again;* my spirit has become *regenerated;* hence, I have the joy of *salvation,* because I am *saved* from the bondage of sin through faith in Christ Jesus. I now stand *justified* before God and therefore reckoned as a *saint* from heaven's perspective. I am now *redeemed* by the precious blood of Jesus Christ from eternal damnation. I have now obtained *Eternal Life."* The use of these words can be deployed mutually to convey almost the same meaning. For instance, if someone says, I am 'Born Again', it practically means he or she has experienced a rebirth; salvation; justification; redemption; regeneration as well as obtained eternal life. All of the aforementioned, makes one a *child of God.* Once a person passes through the phase of rebirth, they become regenerated in their Spirit Man and can be referred to as a child of God. A personal relationship is ensued between such individual and God.

How can I be born again? This is one question that Nicodemus asked Jesus Christ as written in John 3:4 "What do you mean?" exclaimed Nicodemus. "How can an old man go back into his mother's womb and be born again?" This question was in response to a preceding statement made by Jesus Christ, when he said: "I tell you the truth, unless you are born again, you cannot see the kingdom of God." (John 3:3). To be born again, can be defined as the re-birth of the human spirit or the regeneration of the human spirit. Our human spirit resurrects to life as we plant it into the soil of the king of resurrection, our Lord Jesus Christ.

The process of the re-birth to one's spirit is quite simple, yet resulting in the most powerful transformation any human life can ever experience. Therefore, the importance of regeneration can never be over-emphasised in the life of an individual. The re-birth of the human spirit is of utmost importance because everyone born into this world is born into a world of sin, with their spirit severed from the eternal God, hence, without a Godly conscience and power to act Godly. The unregenerated person lives in spiritual defeat because they have the nature of ungodliness in them. The human race is therefore, entangled in a web of disobedience, sin and rebellion against the commandments of God, resulting in a very chaotic world. On the other hand, God hates sin, he deems us as "dead in sins" (Ephesians 2:5) and as "fallen short of his glorious standard." (Romans 3:23). Our sins separate us from God (Isaiah 59:2), and we stand the danger of eternal separation, unless a rebirth occurs in the spirit. (2 Thessalonians 1:7-9). However, God provided a solution, by way of redemption through the shed blood of Jesus Christ.

Jesus Christ came to pay the price. He came to reconcile Man to God. "In whom we have redemption through His blood, the forgiveness of sins, according to the riches of His grace." (Ephesians 1:7). This is 'The rebirth of the human spirit.' - God bringing us out of the condition of spiritual defeat and death to a renewed condition of wholesomeness and Life. When a rebirth occurs in a person's spirit, they become 'Born again' or regenerated in their spirit man. At the point of rebirth, the gift of Eternal Life is being imparted to this person, they receive the Life of Christ, and newness of life occurs in the inward man – The Spirit

Man. Scriptures confirm this reality experience when it says: "This means that anyone who belongs to Christ has become a new person. The old life is gone, a new life has begun." (2 Corinthians 5:17).

In the moment of time that the rebirth of a person's spirit is occurring; a rescuing or salvaging procedure is actually taking place. As the scriptures rightly put it: "For He has rescued us from the kingdom of darkness and transferred us into the kingdom of his dear Son, who purchased our freedom and forgave our sins." (Colossians 1:13-14) Therefore, we have someone who experiences a rebirth of their spirit, and becomes a regenerated person – a New Man, who can now be referred to as the Redeemed or Saved from the kingdom of darkness; initiated into the kingdom of Jesus Christ. This is where the word *'Salvation'* comes from.

When a person is Born Again; it enables them to connect with God's invisible world whilst still living in this present world. At physical death or departure from planet earth, they are assured of arriving in the right place, into God's abode, hence, spending the rest of their life as an eternal being and with a glorified body in God's kingdom. If an individual's spirit is not Born Again, such individual will not be able to experience God's kingdom whilst still living here on earth, and when their physical body dies eventually. This is the truth of the matter.

God's desire is to rescue every single person on the surface of this earth, from the realities of the kingdom of darkness and its characteristics of slavery towards mankind. This world is like a market place where we all come to buy and sell. A place of transaction of which after we are done are sure to return home, but each one of us would have to be the determinant of which home we return to.

The word of God addresses those who have been born-again in their spirit as a prepared and set people to return to a glorious place called heaven, someday after transaction is finished on earth. God in his word referred to these ones as the redeemed. (Ephesians 1:7).

Beloved, the things of the spirit are quite mysterious and sound impossibly foolish to the natural mind, but each one of us must come to the point where we are able to place our trust in God and in his written word.  By doing this, we have nothing to lose, but everything to gain.

# Chapter 6

## IMMUNE PLAN

People do receive some form of protection or another in order to become immune against viable invisible terrible diseases caused by viruses, bacterium or parasites. Getting immunised is one of the ways of escaping the impact of these diseases here on earth. Funnily enough, most of these diseases that we seek to get immunised against are invisible, and many of us have never seen any of these before in our lifetime, but surely, we do believe in the existence of these pathogens partly because of information from scientists and the fact that we do see their manifestations and impacts in human lives from time to time, and so we seek to make every effort to escape the pangs of these unseen agents. Hence, preserving our physical bodies from destruction of these terrible invisible diseases.

It is essential that we do likewise with regards the salvation of our soul, seeking deliverance from eternal destruction because of heaven's information to us through the Word of God; equally warning us, advising us with regards the keeping and preservation of our soul from the pangs of eternal destruction. We are expected to absorb this vital information from God's written Words to us and then make a decision to act upon the voice of the creator of the universe to us, who is trying to show us the right pathway to take. God refers to each one of us in His word as strangers and pilgrims on the earth (Hebrews 11:13), and as such, it makes sense for us to have a look at his map of how we are to journey successfully here on earth physically, mentally and spiritually. Are you already walking on the right spiritual pathway? God in His word reminds his children by saying: "Dear friends, I warn you as temporary residents and foreigners to keep away from worldly desires that wage war against your very soul." (1 Peter 2:11).

When we allow a re-birth of our spirit, it is a kind of immunisation from eternal destruction. We are made righteous and our soul is redeemed from eternal destruction. The application of the sacrificial blood of the Lamb – the shed blood of Jesus Christ is the provision to immunise our spirit and soul from eternal destruction. The potency in the blood is unimaginably powerful and effective to our deliverance.

Jesus Christ is the sacrificial lamb whom God has made as a provision for us in order to escape going through eternal destruction. Eternal destruction is meant for demons, wicked souls and those who reject atonement for their sin. Those who never receive the salvation of their souls will never be able to partake in God's glorious kingdom and will stand the risk of being rejected by heaven on departure from earth. In actual fact, apart from preparing yourself to be able to live successfully on earth, you must never neglect preparing yourself for your future abode outside this present world. We must put into consideration where we would want to spend our life in eternity.

A lifetime spent living under the influence and dictates of self, and not allowing God almighty to have a say in one's life - a lifestyle of sinfulness, living in the opposite direction of God's mandate for one's life; a life not lived in reconciliation with God through our

Lord Jesus Christ could all mean spending eternity in total separation from God.

This is simply the way God has set things out to be and His order of events. However, if an individual becomes regenerated, spending their many days living under the guidance of the Holy Spirit in obedience to the ways of God, they will spend their eternity in the abode of the everlasting God.

We have an arch enemy of our soul, who is a legalist, who will always lay hold on what he believes belong to him. For instance, if a person was so committed to a careless and unguided life, continuously doing those very things which God had said 'thou shall not do' as a result of remaining unregenerate, then when such a life leaves earth, the devil will legally lay claim on such individual as one that died, as an unregenerate human being and in bondage to their sins. Such soul will move into the abode of the lost, totally separated from the love and mercy of God forever.

Hell is formidable, a place of torment. To say that hell is bad is an understatement. It is a place where a soul will cry and lament in agony forever. A place of everlasting separation from God. The final home for the devil and his evil spirits. A place where pleas and repentance are not acknowledged. The Sinners' final destination.

# Chapter 7

## AMAZING LIFE LINE

Jesus Christ defined to us very clearly in the book of John chapter 3:3 that "Truly, truly, I say to you, unless one is born again, he cannot see the kingdom of God." We see from Scriptures how Jesus laid emphasis on the importance of the re-birth of the human spirit. Without the rebirth or regeneration of the human spirit, connectivity with God will be virtually impossible. Let's look at it this way: For the umpteenth time, we need to activate some of our devices or monetary gadgets one way or the other before they can be up and running or before we can use these devices to connect with other people. This might be a secret code, password, or power source. Prior to this, they are dormant or as good as dead. When we follow the manufacturer's guideline in getting our gadgets connected, it all begins to be up and running and that well. When we do otherwise, we get stuck with it. In the same way, God the manufacturer of our spirit, soul and body, already gave us a Manual- The Bible, with its guidelines, informing us on how to get our Spirit Man connected to him in order to come alive. Our individual spirits lay dormant and dead before a re-birth occurs, and so before we are able to connect ourselves with God, our spirit man will have to be activated towards God. God provided a lifeline; a lifeline that will awaken our spirit and enable connectivity Him. That lifeline is Jesus Christ-The Sacrificial Lamb and His shed blood for mankind. This is the way God has set things in place.

A dry corn or bean seed is placed on a shelf for two weeks. In another week's time, it will still remain that one corn or bean seed on a shelf. If it remains on there too long enough, it becomes corrupted and only fit for the bin. On the other hand, once the corn or bean seed is connected to that which will give it life – *the soil*, it springs forth with newness of life. Before his death and resurrection, Jesus Christ said "I tell you the truth, unless a kernel of wheat is planted in the soil and dies, it remains alone. But its death will produce many new kernels – a plentiful harvest of new lives". (John 12:24). Jesus Christ represents that soil in which the life of a human being must be planted in order to receive newness of life. Human beings represent the kernel. Once we get planted in him, and him in us, a re-birth occurs and we regenerate into a new man. He becomes our source of true living. This is why God tells us in his word that "Anyone who belongs to Christ has become a new person. The old life is gone, a new life has begun!" (2 Corinthians 5:17). It is now up to and individual to accept or reject His way of connectivity to Newness of Life.


An unregenerate person is dormant in spirit, but alive in the flesh. God describes such as being dead in sins, with a life experience that will never go beyond the second dimensional life, until it is connected to that which can give it true life. Ephesians 2:5 tells us that "Even though we were dead because of our sins, he gave us life, when he raised Christ from the dead" There is a lifeline involved, and we all need this particular lifeline in order to get our spirit activated. Our true Lifeline is Jesus Christ!

"For God loved the world so much that he gave his one and only Son, so that everyone who believes in him will not perish but have eternal life. God sent his Son into the world not to judge the world, but to save the world through him." (John 3:16). There is undoubtedly going to be an occurrence of 'perishing' unto eternal death, and an occurrence of 'resurrection' unto life eternal. Nevertheless, God gave every single human being the freedom to make a decisive choice of Death or Life.

Many people have always tried other means of connecting to God, but this has invariably made them become entangled in an unnecessary way of religion. Not following the manufacturer's guidelines can make things a whole lot difficult and hard many a times. God made provision in the simplest form. He chose an easy pathway for us. But, why do men choose hard pathways? Many probably don't believe that it can be that simple, but seek pathways where they feel that, God will consider all of their efforts of religious activities and accept them as being good. God helps us to understand in Isaiah 64:6 that "Each of us has become like something unclean, and all our righteous acts are like filthy rags; we all wither like a leaf, and our iniquities carry us away like the wind." God's way is through the shed blood of Jesus Christ. His Word makes us to understand in Hebrew 9:22 that "without the shedding of blood, there is no forgiveness of sins". His way of provision also states in Hebrew 10:19 that "Therefore, brothers since we have confidence to enter the most holy place BY THE BLOOD OF JESUS by the NEW and LIVING way OPENED for us through the curtain of His body."

The most holy place is in the very presence of God; we can only get into the presence of God by way of the blood of Jesus Christ. Even Jesus Christ testified to this truth in John 4:6 when he said: "I am the way, the truth, and the life. No one can come to the Father except through me." Jesus Christ is the password, the code and the bridge that we would need to walk upon in order to get to God.

"For there is one God, and one mediator between God and men, the man Jesus Christ; who gave himself a ransom for all, to be testified in due time." (1 Timothy 2:5). The Word of God in the book of Ephesians 2:14 testify to the fact that "Jesus Christ is our peace, who made both one, and broke down the middle wall of partition". 2 Corinthian 5:18 mentions that "All this is from God, who through Christ reconciled us to himself and gave us the ministry of reconciliation".

When we go through the procedure of re-birth, our connection with God is made sure, fast and secured. Life suddenly becomes like a light bulb that had suddenly become switched on. We are now translated into the invisible kingdom of God. Hence, we begin our new journey in this invisible kingdom – the other side of life!

# Chapter 8

## THE FEAST

There are two kinds of feasts accorded the redeemed or a child of God. The earthly Feast, known as "Our Daily Bread" and the Heavenly Feast known as the "Marriage Feast of the Lamb". The earthly feast is a typical shadow of the heavenly feast. The Heavenly Feast shall take place when the saints are gathered together before the king of kings – Jesus Christ. However, the focus in this book will major on the 'Earthly Feast' but briefly also on the Heavenly Feast, equally referred to as the Banquet.

Regular feasting can occur on a daily basis between a child of God, God the Father, the Son and Holy Spirit on the basis of salvation. There are always no limitations or boundaries as to how much feasting can be done between the child of God and the heavenly triune. The Child of God is always welcome at any time of the day.

Every person who has become Born Again through the rebirth process, enters into a kind of 'regular feasting' with Jesus Christ. This has nothing to do with physical earthly food. "For the kingdom of God is not meat and drink, but righteousness and peace, and joy in the Holy Ghost." (Romans 14:17). His written words in the Bible, to humanity is the first and foremost spiritual Bread that He has prepared for those who would come to dine and wine with Him. This is the reason why scriptures mentioned that: "Man shall not live by bread alone, but by every word that proceeded out of the mouth of God." (Matthew 4:4). His bread is spiritual food and drink for the child of God who is able to draw up strength for life's journey as they feast on it. This can be regarded as a type of spiritual dining and wining with Him. Just as physical food is to the body, so is spiritual food to the Spirit Man; nourishing and invigorating the Spirit Man with vitality.

As children of God, there are so many benefits that can be derived from journeying through God's written word. For instance, through His written word, God- shares His thoughts with His children; making His instructions known to them and bringing correction into their lives. He leads, guides, directs and equips His children for the course ahead. When children of God feast regularly on His word, they are able to gain spiritual strength, insight and authority in the spiritual realm; they are able to hear God's word through His written words; standing upon His promises, His children are able to make demands for supernatural provisions when they pray to Him according to His words. Children of God receive transformation in various aspects of their lives through journeying with God's written words.

Jesus Christ is always constantly knocking at the hearts of millions of unsaved people, inviting them to come and feast with Him: "Behold, I stand at the door and knock: If any man hears my voice, and opens the door, I will come in to him, and will sup with him, and he with me." (Revelation 3:20). Having a sup indicates a type of wining or dinning occasion with somebody. Jesus Christ made use of the word 'sup' to indicate a type of fellowship between him and the invitee. In light of this, Jesus Christ also taught that: "Blessed are they, which do hunger and thirst after righteousness: for they shall be filled." (Mathew 5:6). When Jesus made this statement, He implied that whoever would hunger and thirst after His righteousness would indeed be made righteous in the sight of

God, and would indeed be satisfied. God created humans with a vacuum that needed to be filled with Him. God created each one of us with eternity in mind. It is needful for us to recognise that we all live on the edge of eternity itself. Jesus Christ knew man's desire to fill and satisfy this vacuum; the inner Man or the Spirit Man's, need for its hunger and thirst to be satisfied. However, physical food and physical drink could never have satisfied or quenched such hunger and thirst. The burden bearer - Jesus Christ promised that, as many that would believe in Him would be made satisfied within their Inner Man with the *providence of His own righteousness.*

As children of God, our fellowshipping with Jesus Christ involves becoming a divine partaker of the divine nature of our Lord Jesus Christ. Scriptures tell us: "And because of his glory and excellence, He has given us great and precious promises. These are the promises that enable you to share his divine nature and escape the world's corruption caused by human desires." (2 Peter 1:4). Some of the characteristics of the divine nature of our Lord Jesus Christ that we are able to partake in as children of God include blessings of the fruits of His spirit that enable us to reflect His nature in our lives; receiving the baptism of the Holy Spirit, which empowers us to begin functioning in the supernatural realms of God through Jesus Christ; blessings with spiritual gifts that enable us to move in the supernatural and to also meet the needs of those around us supernaturally; moving from one level of glory to another in the realms of God which empowers us to live constantly as an overcomer, hence living above the evil corruption of this world; receiving the outpouring of His anointing upon our lives which refreshens our entire human existence, which can result in divine health, restoration in many areas of our life, and deliverances from the forces of darkness; receiving revelations from God; enjoyment of His divine presence in our lives; talking to the God, the creator of the universe and Him talking to us;  receiving guidance and directions from God through His Holy Spirit; experiencing His Love, peace, joy, goodness, mercies and many more.  All of these can be referred to as part of our privileges and enjoyments that can be derived from feasting at His table.   However, all of the aforementioned must be obtained by faith in God.  Children of God are equally blessed with heavenly wisdom, knowledge understanding and divine directions, and are able to enjoy heavenly resources that never run dry.  In reality, children of God are meant to run on heaven's economy.  God promised to supply all of our needs according to His riches in glory. (Philippians 4:19). The vastness of the riches of God is immeasurable and cannot be compared with the riches of the world, still yet, 'Faith is the currency that all children of God are expected to have in order to acquire heavens supernatural blessings. The stronger and higher the faith, the more acquisition that can be made of heavenly resources.

Children of God are able to enter God's presence to enjoy sessions of worship before Him, making requests known to Him in prayers with the assurance of answers to prayers.  For the forgoing reason, they are daily and continually loaded with heavenly blessings.  We become Ambassadors to Jesus Christ, and have the potentials of showing forth his goodness – representing His kingdom on earth, as He accords us.

It is worth mentioning, that Jesus Christ by His Holy Spirit does allocate duties of service to His children in various levels of capacities.   In the event of fellowshipping with Jesus Christ, He makes each individual child aware of tasks ahead, and the role He would want each child to play accordingly. Equally, In the course of entertaining each child with His wining and dining, He reveals mysteries to them accordingly and makes known to them His intentions and the role of duty he would want such child to play in the strengthening of God's kingdom.

God's kingdom is highly organised and runs on principles. It runs as a mighty strong force of army. These army are described in God's Word to us as a 'Great and Mighty' with 'Fire burning in front of them' and 'Flames following after them'. 'Looking like horses and charging forward like warhorses', 'Leaping along the mountaintops and making noises like the rumbling of chariots', 'like the roaring of fire, sweeping across a field like stubble, or like a mighty army moving into battle'. The description of their faces is those that grow pale as terror grips them'. 'These army are said as never breaking ranks as they march on, moving in exactly the same position'. 'Breaking through defences without missing a step, they invade as the King of Host of armies directs them', 'The earth quakes' as they advance, the heavens. This army is said to be led by the Lord Jesus Christ Himself, with the army following His orders. (Joel 2:1-11) This is ultimately another entire subject on its own.

In the course of feasting with Jesus Christ, we are strengthened with power and authority by Him and are able to exercise power, authority and dominion over any type of forces of darkness that roam around in the air, land and waters including those attached to human beings. We are able to win every kind of battle through our Lord Jesus Christ. These benefits and many more, are blessings accorded to us when we become children of God and fellowship with Him.

The Marriage Feast of the Lamb is the banqueting that shall take place between the saints (the children of God), referred to as the Bride of Christ and Jesus Christ, referred to as the bridegroom to the saints. There is a set time that this feasting would take place, but the location shall be in the presence of Jesus Christ, at such period, when we shall see Him face to face. It shall be an eternal occurrence. God revealed to us, His intentions when He said "Let us be glad and rejoice, and give honour to Him: for the marriage of the Lamb is come, and His wife has made herself ready. And to her was granted that she should be arrayed in fine linen, clean and white: for the fine linen is the righteousness of saints. And he said unto me, Write, Blessed are they which are called unto the marriage supper of the Lamb. And he said unto me. These are true sayings of God." (Revelation 19:7-9). The redeemed must look forward to this Banquet with great expectation.

It is difficult for the mind of earthly man to comprehend or draw up imaginations on how the heavenly Banquet shall take place. This is the reason why God told us in His Word: "No eye has seen, no ear has heard, and no mind has imagined what God has prepared for those who love him. But it was to us that God revealed these things by his Spirit. For his Spirit searches out everything and shows us God's deep secrets." (1 Corinthians 2:9). Many good-hearted people have come up with various artistic pictures trying to give us imaginations of what it is going to be like. These pictures are fairly nice, but truly have been framed within the earthly imagination of the human mind. In our natural mind, we believe that the banqueting is all going to have to do with food. This is because in our realm, we are only able to relate the word 'Banquet' or 'Supper' with food. The banqueting is going to be way beyond breakfast, lunch or dinner, and possibly may not even involve food.  But we know for sure that it is going to be quite eventful.

Jesus Christ had always likened His great invitations to the human race as a *feast, marriage invite or banquet*.  We can find a typical example of a kind of 'invite' in the book of Mathew chapter 22 Verses 1 to 13.  Right now, as a child of God, you probably feast with Jesus Christ every so often, but it has never involved human physical food.  It has only involved the Bread of Life-   Jesus Christ said: "I am the bread of life.  Whoever comes to me will never be hungry again.  Whoever believes in me will never be thirsty."  This is heavenly bread.  Jesus Christ is the food that endures for eternal life; the true bread of heaven that gives life; spiritual bread that brings eternal life.

Just like the Old Covenant was a shadow to the New Covenant; the Christian Walk on earth is a mirror or shadow of things to come. The banqueting activity is truly beyond earthly or human imagination. Nevertheless, God reveals these mysteries to as many that would walk closely with Him.  Scriptures confirm to us that "The secret of the Lord is with them that fear Him; and he will show them his covenant." (Psalm 25:14).

Taking into account that, our earthly feasting with Jesus Christ has never involved physical feeding and drinking, yet so satisfying and refreshening to the spirit and soul of man, the marriage supper may not necessarily be about having a celebration party; eating drinking, and making merry before Jesus Christ, but may involve much more activities other than just having a sumptuous meal if at all any.  Heaven is filled with so many great activities than we will ever know or imagine with our earthly mind.

# CHAPTER 9

## NEW AND LIVING WAY

A person can only truly become complete, when God fills in the empty space that is vacant in their spirit Man. That empty space belongs to God, and until filled with God almighty, there will never be true satisfaction. Hence, the only way to be complete is through Jesus Christ. Jesus Christ loves each one of us so much and wants to be our number one groom. If you have not yet become His Bride, you can surrender all to Him and ask Him to become your Saviour and Lord and allow him fill the void and make you complete.

Perhaps, you have been questioning and wondering what life is all about. Birth, youth, adulthood, decline and death. Is there no more to life than these? Going to school and obtaining great skills; landing a dream job with a great income; gaining possessions; getting married and having children; eating; sleeping; waking up and attending to daily activities; watching tv; engaging with friends and great activities or hobbies, and invariably repeating these circles of physical life's activities from day-to-day until one day, one grows old and death comes. Life is hugely much more than our mere physical day-to-day activities.

Firstly, Jesus Christ said: "I am come that they might have life, and that they might have it more abundantly." (John 10:10). The 'they' referred to, is to every human being born on earth. The abundant Life spoken of is Eternal Life enjoyed on earth, as a regenerated person. You can only enter into Abundant Life that Jesus Christ offers; as a Regenerated person. It is not a physical life; it is a spiritual life. It is a life of passing from spiritual death to spiritual life.

Dear reader, perhaps you have not yet begun this beautiful journey yet, I am inviting you to make haste, join in and enter this typical Ark of God – His kingdom and the wonders of His glory! It is the most wonderful and glorious journey that God will ever introduce to mankind. It is the unimaginable uttermost blissful journey that any earthly man will ever experience. You can gain life abundance here on earth and gain Eternal Life with God in heaven, after you have left this world. It is possible to gain earthly life and lose one's soul in the event of not becoming regenerated, hence, loosing Eternal Life. Jesus Christ said: "And what shall it profit a man, if he shall gain the whole world, and lose his own soul?" (Mark 8:36).

Having a relationship with God the father, son and his Holy Spirit is the best thing that would ever happen to any man on earth; becoming a partaker of the very life of Jesus in this life and the life thereafter. Come and eat and dine with the King of kings and the Lord of Lords. There is so much in the package of salvation and so much to gain if you are able to take this wonderful step to honour His invitation. God made the way very simple and easy.

# Chapter 10

## THE PROMISE

When we surrender our lives to Jesus Christ, we thereby enter into a beautiful covenant with Him. As we enter into the kingdom of God, it typifies the entering in of the Ark of covenant. Secured in His Ark, and with the experience of turbulences and temptations from the outside world, God promises to see each of His children through to the end. Rest assured that something great lies ahead of you. As you walk closely with Jesus Christ each day, He will cause you to move from one level of glory to another in His kingdom. "Blessed be the God and Father of our Lord Jesus Christ, which according to his abundant mercy has begotten us again unto a lively hope by the resurrection of Jesus Christ from the dead. To an inheritance incorruptible, and undefiled, and that fade not away, reserved in heaven for you." (1 Peter 1:3-4).

As you yield your entire human life to God the father, son and Holy Spirit, you will experience victory over the struggles of your life. God's promise and assurance to us is in His written Words: "Since we have been united with him in death, we will also be raised to life as he was. We know that our sinful selves were crucified with Christ so that sin might lose its power in our lives. We are no longer slaves to sin. For when we died with Christ, we were set free from the power of sin. And since we died with Christ, we know we will also live with him. We are sure of this because Christ was raised from the dead, and he will never die again. Death no longer has any power over him. When he died, he died once to break the power of sin. But now that he lives, he lives for the glory of God. So, you also should consider yourselves to be dead to the power of sin and alive to God through Christ Jesus. Do not let sin control the way you live; do not give in to sinful desire. Do not let any part of your body become an instrument of evil to serve sin. Instead, give yourselves completely to God, for you were dead, but now you have a new life. So, use your whole body as an instrument to do what is right for the glory of God. Sin is no longer your master, for you no longer live under the requirements of law. Instead, you live under the freedom of God's grace." (Romans 6:5-14).

There is always room for growth in the realms of the spirit for the New Believer in Christ. It is therefore, essential for the Inner Man to begin to receive nurturing, so that it can gain the necessary strength it needs. This can be done through constant fellowshipping with God the father, Son and Holy Spirit, through our Lord Jesus Christ. Basically, a new believer must learn to commune with God through prayers; learning His ways by reading scriptures from the Bible. Fellowshipping with other people who have likewise obtained salvation; seeking counsel from those who have been on the journey of salvation in a much longer time than they have been. This is usually the best way to start the journey of salvation. As you walk in this manner with the Lord, you will be moved from one level of glory to another level.

# CHAPTER 11

## THE CALL

"Humans can reproduce only human life, but the Holy Spirit gives birth to spiritual life. So don't be surprised when I say, you must be born again. The wind blows wherever it wants. Just as you can hear the wind but can't tell where it comes from or where it is going, so you can't explain how people are born of the spirit." John 3:6--8.

Our reconciliation with God is now made possible through the shed blood of Jesus Christ. Jesus Christ had paid the final price. His shed blood. It would now be made possible to have Forgiveness and Eternal life "For as many that would believe in Him shall not perish, but have everlasting life" (John 3:16).

**If you would like to become a partaker of God's glorious kingdom, you may wish to use the Prayer Guide outlined in this book to pray.**

Prayer of Salvation:

Oh Lord God, I come to you in the name of Jesus Christ.
I'd love to experience the Rebirth of my spirit.
I'd love to feast with Jesus Christ every day, and for the rest of my life.
I'd love to become your child, almighty God.
Lord Jesus Christ, I receive your invitation and come I come to you.
Reconcile me to God and make every difference there is to my life
Take my sins away, by your precious blood.
Grant me Eternal Life and be my Lord and Saviour.
Write my name in the book of life.
Have mercy upon me and forgive me my sins.
I receive forgiveness, I receive the Love of the Father, Son and Holy Spirit.
Lead me in the pathways of righteousness.
Thank you, heavenly Father. Amen.
I declare that I am saved, I am born again, I am a child of God.
I now have Christ dwelling in me, I am a New Creation Hallelujah!

If you have just said that prayer, congratulations and welcome to God's family. You are now a child of God.

# YOUR SALVATION IS:

## P.R.I.C.E.L.E.S.S

Pure

Rich

Invaluable

Contentment

Eternal

Living

Exquisite

Supernatural

Sure

For more information on how you can grow as a Christian, please contact: info@goodnews-world.org

Please include your prayer requests and comments when you write

Please visit: www.goodnews-world.org

Printed in Great Britain
by Amazon

83625033R00031